TREKKING
IN THE CONGO
RAINFOREST

By Alex Woolf

 Gareth Stevens
PUBLISHING

Please visit our website, **www.garethstevens.com**. For a free color catalog of all our high-quality books, call toll free 1-800-542-2595 or fax 1-877-542-2596

Woolf, Alex.
Trekking in the Congo rainforest / by Alex Woolf.
p. cm. — (Traveling wild)
Includes index.
ISBN 978-1-4824-1327-4 (pbk.)
ISBN 978-1-4824-1253-6 (6-pack)
ISBN 978-1-4824-1509-4 (library binding)
1. Rain forests — Juvenile literature. 2. Rain forest ecology — Juvenile literature. 3. Congo (Democratic Republic) — Juvenile literature. I. Woolf, Alex, 1964-. II. Title.
QH541.5 W63 2015
577.34—d23

Published in 2015 by
Gareth Stevens Publishing
111 East 14th Street, Suite 349
New York, NY 10003

Commissioning editor: Debbie Foy
Designer: Lisa Peacock
Consultant: Michael Scott
Map illustrator: Tim Hutchinson

Picture credits:
PP5, 6: Shutterstock; P7 Cyril Ruoso/FLPA; P8, 9: Shutterstock; P10 Ingo Arndt/FLPA; P11 Andy Rouse/naturepl.com; P12 Martin Harvey/Corbis; P13 Martin Harvey/Photoshot; P14 Shutterstock; P15 Martyn Colbeck/Oxford Scientific/Getty; P16 Graeme Williams/Photoshot; P17T Shutterstock; P17B Martin Harvey/Getty Images; P18 Shutterstock; P19T R&M Van Nostrand/FLPA; P19B Shutterstock; P20T Martin Harvey/Getty Images; P20B Cyril Ruoso/FLPA; P21 Graeme Williams/Photoshot; P22, 23B Shutterstock; P23T Jacques Jangoux/Photoshot; P24 Martin Harvey/Getty Images; P25T Robert Harding photo; P25B Shutterstock; P26 AF P/Getty Images; P27T Cyril Ruoso/FLPA; P28 Eric Baccega/naturepl.com; P29 Mitsuaki Iwago/Getty Images. All incidental images by Shutterstock..

Printed in the United States of America

CPSIA compliance information: Batch CS15GS: For further information contact Gareth Stevens, New York, New York at 1-800-542-2595.

CONTENTS

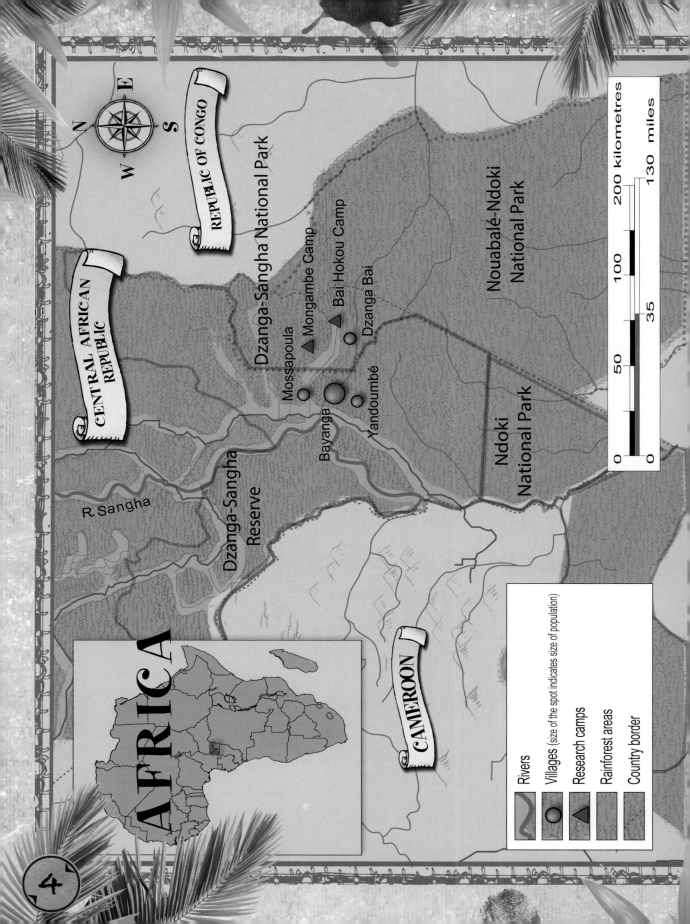

REPUBLIC OF CONGO

CENTRAL AFRICAN REPUBLIC

Dzanga-Sangha National Park

▲ Mongambe Camp

▲ Bai Hokou Camp

Mossapoula

Bayanga

Yandoumbé

Dzanga Bai

Nouabalé-Ndoki National Park

Ndoki National Park

R. Sangha

Dzanga-Sangha Reserve

CAMEROON

AFRICA

200 kilometres

130 miles

100

35

50

0

0

Rivers

Villages (size of the spot indicates size of population)

Research camps

Rainforest areas

Country border

THE CONGO RAINFOREST

Preparing for the trip

This is so exciting! I'm heading off to the Congo rainforest in central Africa. For ten days, I'll be trekking through the jungle, observing the wildlife, and meeting some of the indigenous people. There are bound to be dangers: snakes and spiders, not to mention hippos and gorillas! But I'm sure it'll be an unforgettable experience.

The heart of darkness

The Congo rainforest is the second largest in the world, spreading through six countries and covering 695,000 square miles (1,800,000 sq km). Only the Amazon is bigger. The rainforest teems with life, with more than 600 tree species and 10,000 animal and bird species, including forest elephants, chimpanzees, and peacocks.

My destination

I'll be staying at the Dzanga–Sangha Reserve in southwestern Central African Republic. It's a protected area of tropical rainforest covering 2,650 square miles (6,865 sq km). It was established in 1990 and is one of several reserves that together make up the Dzanga–Sangha Complex of Protected Areas. The main river running through the reserve is the Sangha River. Average annual rainfall in the reserve is about 59 inches (1,500 mm) and the average temperature is 75–84°F (24–29°C). The map opposite shows its location.

Equipment

I've decided to bring the following:
- sturdy walking boots
- sandals
- shorts and pants
- long-sleeved shirts (to protect against mosquitoes and creepers)
- backpack
- machete
- compass
- first aid kit (including antimalarial pills)
- insect repellent
- rain gear
- water bottle
- hat
- basic fishing equipment

MY ARRIVAL

Day 1, June 8
Bayanga

This morning, a small propeller plane flew me from the international airport at Bangui, the capital of Central African Republic, to the village of Bayanga (see map on page 4). We flew over an endless green carpet of forest before touching down on a modest airstrip. The jungle heat and humidity struck me powerfully as I stepped off the plane. Bayanga isn't quite the traditional place I'd been expecting, with all the cars and motorbikes whizzing around its streets. The houses may have palm-tree roofs, but many also sprout satellite dishes.

Bayanga village

The largest settlement in the Dzanga–Sangha Reserve began as a simple fishing village on the banks of the Sangha River. In the 1970s a sawmill opened there, and the village's population swelled as migrant workers arrived from all parts of the country. When the reserve was established in 1990, it provided further job opportunities for locals. The BaAka forest people come into the village to trade their bushmeat and honey for manioc and other farm produce.

The Sangha River is the main waterway flowing through the Dzanga-Sangha Reserve. Local people use it for fishing, washing clothes, and transportation.

Be smart, survive!

I watched in amazement as the BaAka people built a rainforest shelter from branches and palm fronds. Here's how:

1. Find two forked tree branches and plant them firmly in the ground roughly about 6.5 feet (2 m) apart.
2. Find several long, thin, flexible branches and cut these to the same length. Bend them so that both ends are planted in the ground, forming a row of arches between the upright branches.
3. Run another set of thin branches lengthwise along the arches, attaching them with liana vines, to create a lattice.
4. Cover your lattice structure with palm fronds to create a rainproof shelter.

The BaAka

These are the indigenous people of the rainforests of southwestern Central African Republic. They also live in parts of Cameroon, Republic of Congo, and Gabon. They obtain everything they need from the forest. The men hunt and trap using poisoned darts and spears, and obtain honey from beehives. The women gather wild fruits and nuts and natural medicines.

EXPLORING THE RAINFOREST

Day 2, June 9

I spent today exploring the rainforest, looking for local sources of water, observing the wildlife... and getting wet. The rain was unrelenting! When it finally stopped, the temperature shot up and I became soaked with sweat - altogether a very wet experience! It is beautiful here, though, and so rich in wildlife. I spotted brightly colored butterflies and beetles, a group of buffalo, and a gorgeous red-furred sitatunga antelope with her fawn.

Rainforest climate

Like all tropical rainforests, the Congo basin is warm and humid. It rains about 117 days per year, with a total of approximately 70 inches (1,766 mm) of rainfall. The heaviest rains fall between March and November. During the day, temperatures vary between 68 and 81°F (20 and 27°C), while night temperatures average 59°F (15°C).

Life in the rainforest

In any 4-square-mile (10 sq km) area of the African rainforest, you can find hundreds of species of birds, insects, mammals, and amphibians, including the rock python, chimpanzee, pygmy hippo, colobus monkey, and the termite. Many of these cannot be found anywhere else in the world. It's estimated that there are only 3,000 pygmy hippos left in the wild. The African rainforest is similarly diverse in terms of plant species. Around 800 plant types have been identified so far, but this may be just 10% of the total.

Rainforest structure

Tropical rainforests have layers, each with their own ecosystem.

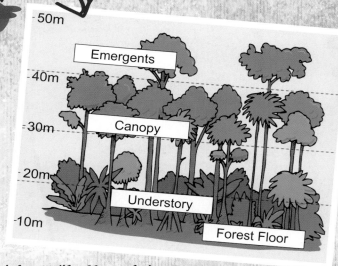

- Forest floor: Very little sunlight means that hardly anything grows. Dead leaves and plants decompose into the thin topsoil, and their nutrients are absorbed by the trees.
- Understory: Dark and humid, the lower part of the canopy is teeming with insect life. The leaves are big and broad to catch what little light gets through.
- Canopy: This is home to the majority of rainforest life. Many of the monkeys, reptiles, birds, and insects that live here rarely visit the ground.
- Emergents: This layer comprises the tallest trees of the rainforest, growing as high as 164 feet (50 m) above the ground.

Leeches

GET OUT ALIVE!!

After washing in the river today a leech attached itself to my toe and began to feed on my blood! Never pull a leech off as this can tear your skin and lead to infection. Instead use a flat, blunt object to gently break the seal around its mouth and it will drop off.

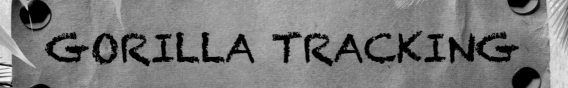

GORILLA TRACKING

Day 3, June 10

I'm with a party of researchers, following a BaAka guide through the forest. Now and again, he'll stop and study the ground, looking for telltale signs of the western lowland gorilla such as broken branches or disturbed leaves. Suddenly, he motions to us to stop. He points toward a clearing up ahead. To my delight I see a family of five gorillas!

Finding and observing

At sunrise each morning, a team of researchers, led by a BaAka guide, leaves Bai Hokou camp (see map on page 4) and heads for the spot where the gorillas slept the previous night. Once the nest site is found, the team follows the subtle trail the gorillas left while moving and feeding. Hours may go by before the gorillas are found, usually relaxing near a fruit tree. As well as fruit, they eat roots, shoots, tree bark, insects, and small reptiles.

Great apes of the forest

Western lowland gorillas live in groups of up to 30. They are led by an older adult male, called the silverback, who organizes group activities such as eating, nesting, and moving around. If anyone challenges the silverback, he can become very aggressive, standing up, roaring, charging, and pounding his chest. Young gorillas behave much like children, spending their days playing, climbing trees, and chasing one another.

What if a gorilla charges at you?

If a gorilla charges at you, crouch down slowly and make yourself look as small as possible. Don't look at the gorilla. These submissive gestures will make the gorilla understand that you offer no threat. Do not run. The guide will ask you to move slowly away.

Conservation

Western lowland gorillas are now regarded as critically endangered. Their numbers have been greatly reduced over recent decades due to habitat loss, disease, and hunting. These gorillas are a protected species and it is illegal to hunt them. However, it is not easy for the authorities to stop the hunters. Rainforest people have hunted small numbers of gorillas for centuries using traditional techniques. Today, gorillas are vulnerable to commercial hunters using high-powered rifles. Roads built by logging companies have given hunters ever greater access to the forest, further threatening these animals.

WATCHING THE FOREST ELEPHANTS

Day 4, June 11
Dzanga Bai

Today we walked to Dzanga Bai, a large forest clearing (see map on page 4). To my amazement, there were more than 80 forest elephants there. We climbed a wooden platform to watch without disturbing them. They ranged from large adult males to very young calves keeping close to their mothers. We saw them raising their trunks, scenting new arrivals, and greeting each other by touching heads, while the calves chased each other around, splashing in the water like children.

Gentle giants

African forest elephants live in the rainforests of the Congo basin. Though smaller than the African bush elephant, males can reach up to 10 feet (3 m) in height, and their tusks can grow to nearly 5 feet (1.5 m). They use these long tusks to dig for roots in the ground, strip bark off trees, defend themselves from predators, and fight with other males during the mating season. Males tend to be solitary, but females and their young form family groups called herds. Forest elephants communicate by making sounds so low, humans can't even hear them.

Dzanga Bai's precise location is largely unknown, perhaps to deter poachers.

When elephants attack!

Forest elephants are generally shy, but if they are disturbed when feeding, for example, they can become aggressive. If the elephant begins shaking its head, that usually means it's about to charge. If its ears are sticking out, it's probably a mock charge. If they're pinned back, you should be worried. Running will not help as they are very fast. Climb a tree or throw a decoy such as your hat or shirt.

Dzanga Bai

This large forest clearing is popular with local wildlife because the soil is rich in minerals. Animals find these minerals in the stagnant surface water and by digging holes in the ground. Elephants need the nutrients from the minerals to help them reproduce. Since 1990, researchers have studied more than 4,000 elephants at Dzanga Bai and have learned a great deal about their behavior.

Be smart, survive!

Animals can often lead a rainforest trekker to water. Birds flying straight and low around dawn and dusk are usually heading for water. If they're flying from tree to tree, resting frequently, they're returning from a drink. Bees seldom travel more than 3.7 miles (6 km) from water, and a column of ants marching up a tree are heading for a reservoir of trapped water.

THE SALINES

Day 5, June 12

Mbanda and I have spent the day hiking along elephant paths - the only practical way of crossing this dense forest. Mbanda is a BaAka guide. I feel safe with him as he knows the forest well. He led me through a series of forest clearings crossed by streams, called salines, where wild animals often gather to forage. We spotted bongo antelopes, giant forest hogs, and storks. We had to leave the salines by dusk, because Mbanda said that is when the forest elephants come, and it could be dangerous. At night we stayed in the Bai Hokou camp.

Bongo

These large forest antelopes have beautiful coats of deep chestnut with white stripes to camouflage them from predators. They have large, spiraled horns that they lay on their backs when they run through the forest, so they don't get caught on the branches. The males use their horns to spar with each other, but this is like a ritual — injuries are rare. Timid and easily frightened, these nocturnal creatures can move at great speed to escape predators, even through dense undergrowth.

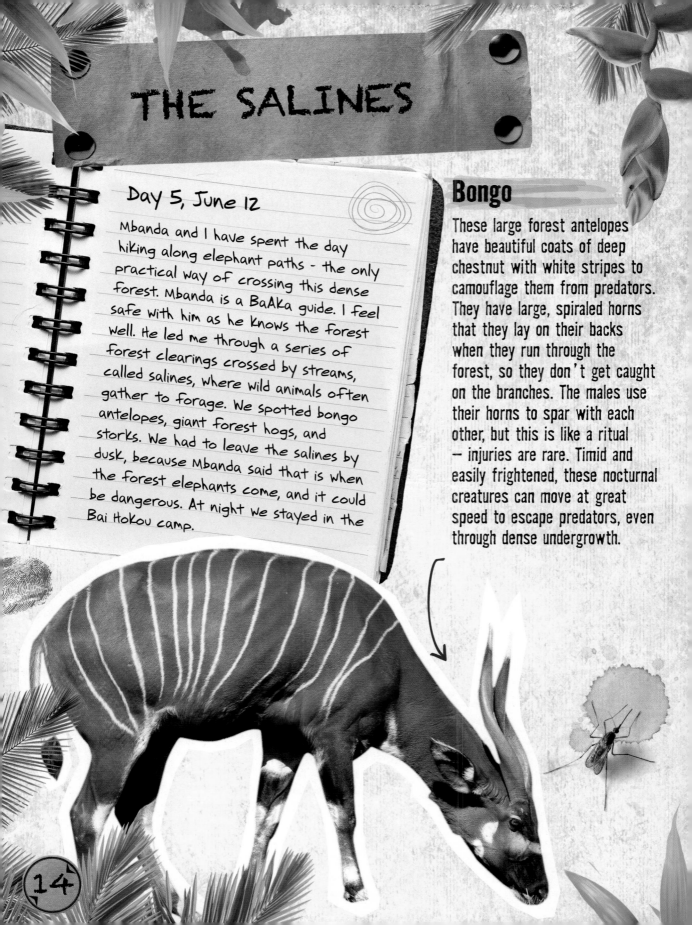

Snakes!

Many dangerous snakes live in the Congo rainforest:

- The Gaboon viper is cream and brown, and lives on the forest floor. It has the longest fangs and highest venom yield of any snake!
- The forest cobra is the world's biggest cobra, growing up to 10 feet (3 m) in length. It can be found hiding among logs, tree roots, or rock crevices.
- The black mamba is greatly feared. It can travel at up to 12 miles (19 km) per hour and its bite can kill a human in four hours.

Giant forest hog

These are just babies below, but giant forest hogs are the largest of all wild pigs and can grow to over 6.5 feet (2 m) long with tusks of up to 13.8 inches (35 cm). Although hogs are herbivores, sometimes they scavenge dead animals. Hogs live in herds of up to 20, called sounders. They are feared in the rainforest, as males sometimes attack without warning, possibly to protect the sounder. Males have also been known to fight each other to the death!

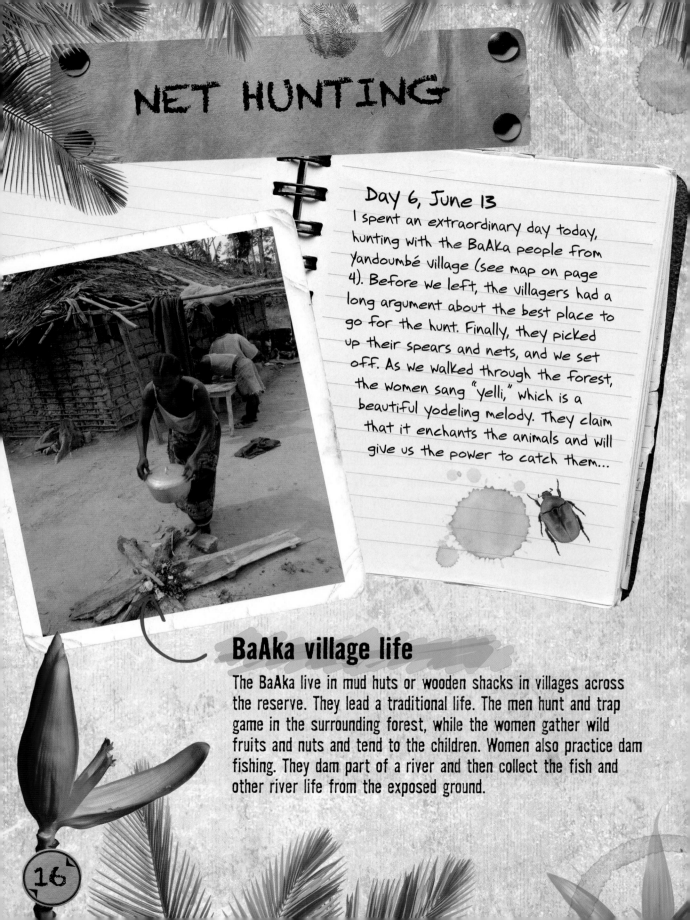

NET HUNTING

Day 6, June 13

I spent an extraordinary day today, hunting with the BaAka people from Yandoumbé village (see map on page 4). Before we left, the villagers had a long argument about the best place to go for the hunt. Finally, they picked up their spears and nets, and we set off. As we walked through the forest, the women sang "yelli," which is a beautiful yodeling melody. They claim that it enchants the animals and will give us the power to catch them...

BaAka village life

The BaAka live in mud huts or wooden shacks in villages across the reserve. They lead a traditional life. The men hunt and trap game in the surrounding forest, while the women gather wild fruits and nuts and tend to the children. Women also practice dam fishing. They dam part of a river and then collect the fish and other river life from the exposed ground.

Natural materials

The BaAka use long nets, called kusa, made from strips of liana bark. The women carry baskets, known as ikwa, made from fibers of the raffia palm. The hunt I went on took place close to the village, but at other times of year hunters may head much deeper into the forest. They build camps out of forest materials, and can remain there for months on end.

Jungle eye

GET OUT ALIVE!!

To move safely through the rainforest, you must develop a "jungle eye." Don't look at the bushes and trees immediately in front of you. Focus instead on the vegetation 10–20 feet (3–6 m) ahead and check for natural breaks in the foliage. Look through the jungle, not at it. Occasionally check the rainforest floor for animal trails that may lead you to water.

In BaAka culture, hunting is one of the most important activities and hunters are highly respected.

Catching the animals

Once they've reached their destination, the hunters form a semicircle and tie their nets to low branches and lianas, keeping them out of sight. Then several men rush forward screaming and pounding the ground with branches, hoping to drive gazelles and antelopes into the nets. A blow to the head kills the animal instantly. On the return journey, the women collect leaves and nuts to accompany the meat. The meat is divided between all the villagers, with the best parts going to the catcher. Other animals hunted include crocodiles, monkeys, elephants, and the pangolin, an insect-eating mammal like an anteater covered with scales.

RIVER LIFE

Day 7, June 14

Today, I took a trip down the Sangha River (see map on page 4) in a pirogue, or dugout canoe, and checked out some of the amazing bird life in this area. I was very impressed with the skill of Jafaru, my piroguier (canoe-man), standing upright at the stern of the boat as he navigated us through some strong currents. On our trip along the Sangha and its tributary, the Mossapoula, we spotted kingfishers, eagles, and even caught a glimpse of the very rare Hartlaub duck.

Sangha River

The Sangha is a tributary of the Congo River, which flows south through the Dzanga–Sangha Reserve. The Sangha River flows 140 miles (225 km) south to Ouesso in Republic of Congo and forms part of Cameroon's border with the Central African Republic and Republic of Congo. The river then twists an additonal 225 miles (362 km) to its mouth on the Congo River, south of Bobaka.

Bird life

There are 379 known bird species in the Dzanga–Sangha Reserve. These include residents, like the goliath heron and the African fish eagle, which are here all year round. There are also many visitors from North Africa, Europe, and Asia, such as the Eurasian kestrel and grey–headed gull, as well as visitors from other parts of sub–Saharan Africa, like the long–tailed cormorant and giant kingfisher.

The Congo peafowl lives in the lowland forests of the Congo River Basin.

Aquatic life

The river contains more than 60 fish species and a large population of shrimp, harvested by the local people. There are also fierce animals in its waters, including crocodiles and hippos, and the goliath tigerfish, which is a sharp–toothed predator that grows to 5 feet (1.5 m) and has been known to attack humans.

Be smart, survive!

Hippos are responsible for more human deaths in Africa than any other large animal. Here are some tips in case you come across one:

1. If a hippo is sniffing the ground, it's looking for food, so give it some space!
2. On land, never get between a hippo and the water.
3. In a boat, be careful not to hit a hippo with your oar. The hippo could overturn your boat or even bite it in two!
4. Avoid hippos at night, when they're most alert.
5. If a hippo charges at you, run among trees and rocks as they will slow the hippo down.

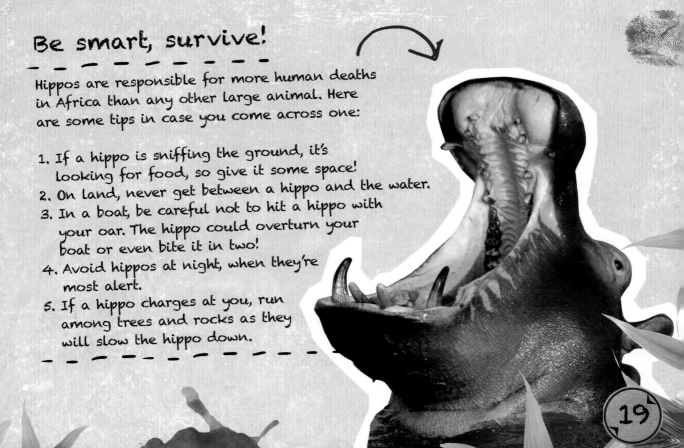

COLLECTING PLANTS AND HONEY

Day 8, June 15

I spent today with the BaAka men and women from Mossapoula on an excursion into the forest. I watched in awe as a man climbed 130 feet (40 m) up a tree with nothing but an ax and a liana vine, braving stinging bees, to collect honey from their hives. Later, I observed women gathering leaves and extracting sap for medicine. It was incredible to see the efforts they made to obtain things that I would normally get from a supermarket or pharmacy.

Collecting honey

The BaAka men who collect honey are among the most respected in the village. It is a dangerous process, and many men die. The honey collector climbs the tree by using an ax to cut notches for footholds and wrapping a liana vine around himself and the trunk as a harness. When he reaches the crown of the tree, he leaves the safety of his harness and walks carefully along a narrow branch to the nest. Now the bees start to attack, and he must get to the honey before he is overcome by their stings. He uses a smoking branch to distract the bees, but he still gets stung. After hacking through the branches to the hive, he removes the honeycomb. The BaAka use honey as a sweetener, and they also eat it straight from the comb. It is considered a great delicacy.

Poisonous plants

When foraging in the Congo rainforest, avoid the following plants:

- plants with white or yellow berries
- mushrooms – some are safe but many are toxic
- plants with thorns
- plants with shiny leaves
- plants with leaves in groups of three
- plants with umbrella-shaped flowers

To be absolutely safe, do not eat any plant unless you are sure it's edible!

GET OUT ALIVE!!

Medicines of the forest

The medical knowledge of the BaAka is passed from mother to daughter. The women know exactly what plants have healing qualities. They use their machetes for all sorts of tasks, from cracking nuts to scraping powder from the inside of bark. Leaves are pressed to extract sap, or rolled into a funnel to apply medicine to the ears or eyes. The forest provides them with medicines for worms, malaria, snakebites, and many other ailments.

These women grow manioc and bananas. They work communally, often singing as they work.

21

MONKEY WALK

Day 9, June 16

Today I spent time at the Mongambe camp (see map on page 4) and trekked through the rainforest with a large group of agile mangabey monkeys! They have become used to having humans around, and it's amazing to watch them rummage through leaf litter for insects, raid birds' nests for eggs, crack open nuts with their powerful jaws, groom each other, and make raucous whoops that echo across the entire forest!

Agile mangabeys

Unlike many monkeys, the agile mangabey spends a lot of its time on the ground, making it easy to observe. In 2004, the World Wildlife Fund for Nature selected a group of more than 200 and began getting them used to people, so that scientists could observe them closely. Today, this group is happy to be followed around the forest by researchers and tourists. They can be seen eating, fighting, playing, and even hunting young antelopes.

Be smart, survive!

Insects are a good source of protein, and easier to catch than larger animals. An experienced traveler could easily survive for months on a diet of beetles, worms, grubs, and termites.

A woman of the Libinza tribe prepares to cook a meal of grubs.

Snakebite!

If you are bitten by a snake:
- check if the snake is venomous (venomous snakebites will show puncture marks, pain, redness, and swelling)
- stay calm, keep the wound below your heart, and avoid exertion, to reduce the flow of venom around your body
- call for medical help. Note the snake's markings to help identify it, so the correct antivenom can be prescribed.

GET OUT ALIVE!!

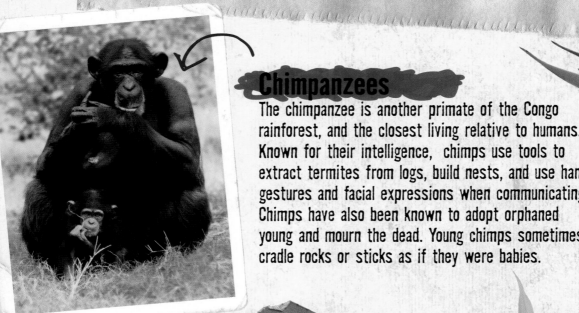

Chimpanzees

The chimpanzee is another primate of the Congo rainforest, and the closest living relative to humans. Known for their intelligence, chimps use tools to extract termites from logs, build nests, and use hand gestures and facial expressions when communicating. Chimps have also been known to adopt orphaned young and mourn the dead. Young chimps sometimes cradle rocks or sticks as if they were babies.

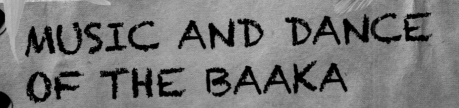

MUSIC AND DANCE OF THE BAAKA

Day 10, June 17

The last evening of my trip was spent in the village of Mossapoula, enjoying the traditional songs, percussion, and dancing of the BaAka people. It was a magical experience that I'll never forget. The BaAka dancers shook and swayed, and I lost myself in the fast, energetic rhythms. Everyone took part, from young children to the elderly, banging sticks on buckets, clapping, and shaking branches. What a way to end my trip!

BaAka culture

After a successful hunt, the BaAka people use music and dance to express their thanks to the forest spirit they call *Jengi*. The dance is called *Luma* and is accompanied by drumming and singing. The singing involves several different melodies that harmonize with each other. The BaAka people also perform music and dance to celebrate important stages in people's lives, such as weddings, funerals, and a boy's passage into adulthood.

Women and dance

Just as BaAka women play an important role in gathering plants and fishing, they are often center stage in the dances. The *ginda*, or master of the dance, can be played by either a man or a woman. There are also female-only dances, such as *Dingboku* and *Elamba*—when one woman dances solo. They dance in skirts made of raffia and leaves.

BaAka girls perform a coming-of-age ceremony.

Threats to the BaAka

Today, the BaAka's traditional way of life is threatened by changes to the rainforest. Multinational logging and mining companies are clearing large expanses of forest, including BaAka areas. Also, the population of the region has swelled due to the arrival of refugees from local conflicts, and unemployed migrant workers. The incomers clear more forest to create plantations. As the forests shrink, the animals hunted by the BaAka disappear. The conservation movement may have added to the problem by pushing for a ban on the hunting of forest animals, turning the BaAka into criminals.

Repelling insects

Insects are a constant irritation in the rainforest, and can also carry disease. Insect repellent is a must, but here are some other ways to keep insects at bay:

- Tie a T-shirt over your head and let it hang down over your neck.
- Rub mud on your exposed skin. Once it dries, it will form a crusty barrier against insects.
- Build a campfire. Its smoke will ward off insects at dawn and dusk.

THREATS TO THE FOREST

Day 11, June 18

I packed up camp this morning, said goodbye to my BaAka friends, and boarded the propeller plane to take me back to Bangui. We flew over the rainforest canopy, and I saw roads carved through the trees by commercial logging companies. We passed over breaks in the forest where the trees had been burned to blackened stumps. In other cleared areas we saw piles of logs beside trucks and bulldozers. It was a powerful reminder of the threats faced by the rainforest.

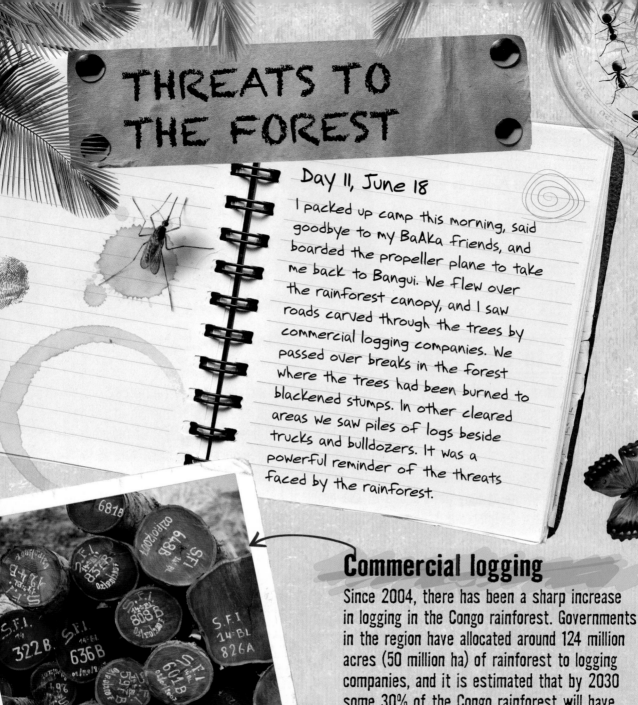

Commercial logging

Since 2004, there has been a sharp increase in logging in the Congo rainforest. Governments in the region have allocated around 124 million acres (50 million ha) of rainforest to logging companies, and it is estimated that by 2030 some 30% of the Congo rainforest will have disappeared, unless action is taken to stop deforestation. Logging roads open up the forests, bringing new settlers from other areas, some of whom carry diseases to which the indigenous tribes have no immunity. The logging industry provides thousands of jobs for the local people, so there are no simple solutions.

Bushmeat

Poachers use the logging roads to hunt forest animals and sell this "bushmeat" to loggers and villagers. Many animals, such as monkeys and elephants, have been slaughtered for the bushmeat trade. Elephants face an additional threat from poachers who hunt them for their tusks.

Slash-and-burn agriculture

Once the loggers have moved on, the roads they leave provide access for small farmers. They "slash and burn" more of the forest and use the cleared spaces to grow crops. But rainforest soil is poor in nutrients and quickly depleted, so the farmers move ever deeper into the forest and repeat the process.

Dealing with ticks

GET OUT ALIVE!!

Ticks are small, round bloodsuckers that spread diseases, some fatal. You have roughly six hours from the tick's attachment to catching any disease it may be carrying, so check for ticks regularly! Try to remove the whole tick (with mouthparts still attached) with a gloved hand, clean fingers, or with tweezers if you have them.

WHAT CAN I DO?

Parting thoughts

On my flight back to Bangui, I reflected on the incredible time I'd just spent in Dzanga-Sangha Reserve. It seems that the Central African Forest Commission, with help from conservation groups like the World Wildlife Fund for Nature, have done a fantastic job of preserving this unique habitat and protecting it from poachers, loggers, miners, and other threats. But I'm worried about the rest of the Congo rainforest, and I've started to wonder what I can do to help protect it.

A global problem

Despite global concern, rainforests continue to be destroyed at a rate of over 79,000 acres (32,000 ha) per day. Many species have become extinct and the traditional way of life for millions of rainforest people is under threat. Rainforests also affect the global climate. They help bring about regular rainfall, preventing floods and droughts. They produce oxygen, which we need to breathe, and absorb huge quantities of carbon dioxide, a gas that contributes to global warming. Destroying the rainforests threatens life on this planet!

Hope for the future

We can help save the rainforests by putting pressure on our governments to act and by living in a way that doesn't harm the environment. Farmers who slash and burn the rainforests to grow crops need to be encouraged to try more sustainable forms of agriculture. Governments should support and encourage companies that operate in ways that minimize damage to the rainforests.

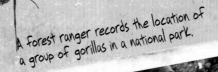

A forest ranger records the location of a group of gorillas in a national park.

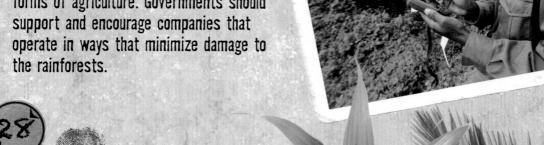

Taking action

Action is already being taken by conservation groups and aid agencies. They are working with forest communities to show them how valuable their forests can be as tourist areas. In the Democratic Republic of Congo, a charity called Rainforest Foundation UK is working with forest dwellers from 100 villages to help them produce detailed maps of their location. This will prove the ownership of the land to loggers and to the government, helping to prevent deforestation in those areas.

For a different view of the Congo rainforest, these tourists are taking a ride in a hot-air balloon.

GLOSSARY

adze A tool similar to an ax with an arched blade at right angles to the handle, used for cutting or shaping large pieces of wood.

bushmeat The meat of African wild animals.

camouflage An animal's coloring or shape that enables it to disguise itself by blending in with its surroundings.

canopy The dense layer of leaves high above the ground in a forest.

carbon dioxide A colorless, odorless gas produced by burning carbon-containing materials, such as wood, vegetable matter, and gasoline.

decompose To decay naturally (for plant and animal matter), releasing goodness back into the soil.

deforestation The clearance of rainforests.

depleted Used up.

ecosystem A community of interacting organisms and the physical environment around them.

eddy A circular movement of water, going against the main current, causing a small whirlpool.

extinction The state or process of being wiped out.

foliage Tree or plant leaves.

forage Search for food.

frond The leaf-like part of a palm or similar plant.

global warming The gradual increase in the overall temperature of Earth's atmosphere, caused partly by human activities.

habitat The natural home or environment of an animal or plant.

herbivore An animal that feeds on plants.

humidity The amount of water vapor in the atmosphere.

indigenous Native to an area.

leech A worm-like, bloodsucking creature.

liana A woody climbing plant that hangs from trees in tropical rainforests.

logging The cutting down of trees for timber.

machete A broad, heavy knife.

malaria An often deadly disease of tropical and subtropical regions, transmitted by mosquitoes.

migrant Someone who moves from place to place to live.

nocturnal Creatures that are active at night.

nutrients Nourishment.

percussion Musical instruments played by striking with the hand or with a stick of some kind.

poacher A person who hunts animals or fish illegally.

rainforest A dense forest, rich in plant and animal life, with consistently heavy rainfall, usually found in tropical areas.

sap The fluid that circulates within plants.

sawmill A factory in which logs are sawed into planks by machine.

submissive To show obedient and humble behavior.

sub-Saharan Africa The part of Africa that is immediately south of the Sahara Desert.

sustainable In a way that minimizes damage to the environment.

tarpaulin Heavy-duty waterproof cloth.

tick A bloodsucking relative of the spider.

topsoil The richer, upper layer of soil.

venom Poisonous fluid secreted by animals such as snakes, spiders, and scorpions.

worms A general slang term for parasites of the intestines. A parasite is an animal or plant that lives and feeds on another (host) organism.

INDEX & FURTHER INFORMATION

Books

Find Out About Rainforests, Jen Green (Armadillo Books, 2013)
Rainforest Destruction (Mapping Global Issues), Peter Littlewood (Watts, 2012)
Rainforests (Eco Alert) by Rebecca Hunter (Franklin Watts, 2012)

Websites

http://www.dzanga-sangha.org
http://rainforests.mongabay.com/congo/
http://worldwildlife.org/places/congo-basin